Relationships with God

Doug Stephenson

Cover Image Claire Williams

Cover Layout Teri Crawford

Indian Edition

FOR YOU

INTRODUCTION

For millennia, human beings have had a relationship with an invisible spiritual energy, a Divine source, known by as many names as there are languages and cultures of the world. This indescribable Mystery of the universe has intrigued us for a very long time. What if it was possible to know this Being we call God, personally and directly?

There are saints, holy people and prophets who have shared their personal experience inviting us into a closer connection with God. But what if we also, could have a direct and personal relationship with this Source?

In this book, writer, gardener, and meditator Doug Stephenson shares his personal and intimate reflections on his experience with the Divine Source. Gently, like opening a box of treasures, he has quietly dedicated his life to knowing God, knowing himself and exploring the mysteries of this Being. I hope you enjoy this beautiful sharing.

Imagine a huge, unlimited space far beyond this world of time, matter, and action: a world of golden silence; not a drop of sound; no hands of time directing existence; a land of permanent peace and freedom. This is the world of eternity; silent and unchanging.

In this world lives a point of conscient energy, eternally bodiless; a pure being who calls this world 'Home'. This point of pure, benevolent and all-knowing energy radiates light. This is the Alpha Point. This is God.

Anthony Strano, The Alpha Point

God as My Companion

You have chosen me to be your companion, to share this journey with You. Why?

You already know me so well; You know what I will bring to the relationship, to the journey. You tell me it is because what we have in common is so much more than what we differ on; we are on the same wavelength; there exists an equality.

My own starting point is somewhat different: all of this I have yet to discover for myself and believe in. Consequently, as the journey begins, I find I express myself in one of two ways, neither of which are mirrored in Your calm certainty. The first is an almost uncontrolled rush of energy to experience and share with You. This is like a bottle of champagne being uncorked, which froths over in a release of enthusiasm, eventually to be replaced by a gentler rising of bubbles to the surface.

The second manner is one of uncertainty; not being sure how I will be received. This is like the overly tall and ungainly child who, when asked to partake in some sports event, is initially unsure of their coordination and so holds back until they have gained confidence in their ability.

I am both

However, as my Companion, You respectfully acknowledge my different energies as I attempt to establish parameters, define the relationship and find my/our balance.

As time passes, I begin to revel in Your companionship: You stimulate me, You challenge me, You introduce new depths to my thinking. As we explore the unfolding journey together, You give meaning to the passing scenes, to the various experiences, to the highs and lows. If our opinions differ, we explore those difference together while maintaining respect for one another.

I find You to be both funny and serious, a good listener and an informative contributor, detached and fully engaged. You show that You know me well enough to gauge my mood – what not to say, as well as what to say and when to say it.

Focus your smart phone camera on this QR code to link directly to a guided meditation commentary on YouTube

God as My Guide

One doesn't become a guide just because you know the way: you achieve this qualification because you have sensitivity to the needs, the fears and perhaps the over-confidence of those whom you take within your care.

As my Guide, You prepare me for the journey ahead: You inspire me with a sense of challenge, You engage me in imagery of what will be experienced on the way and You caution me as to when and how pitfalls may be encountered.

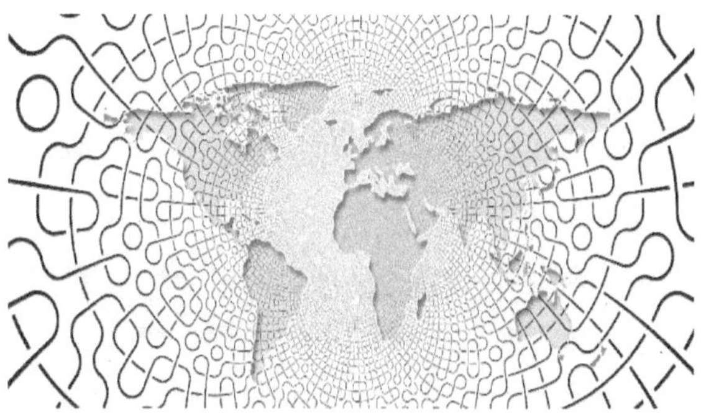

As the journey begins, there is a lightness in my

step as my mind remains free from the need to check which is the right direction. Because You are with me and You have shown to me many times before that You are so familiar with the path, I need not concern myself with such questions: I can give my attention to the unfolding experience.

There are times, when the route is less clearly defined, that You take the lead, attentively indicating how best to traverse the difficulty. At other times, when the path is obvious and easy, You walk with me or even behind me. Such carefree moments are both a counter-balance to the more challenging times as well as an opportunity to reflect on the successes to date. I sense that You know just when to introduce such moments such that my confidence grows as a result.

Because You know the journey from its beginning through the middle to the end, as well as recognizing my capabilities, You are in a position to indicate appropriate pace, places to recharge ones energies and so how to take maximum enjoyment from the journey.

Your role as my Guide, through gentle management of my time and energies, is to enable me to reach the destination safely, while having enjoyed a rich, diverse, and deeply profound collage of experiences. This You do in such a manner that it maximizes my own sense of achievement while allowing Your gently supportive role to fade into the background.

Focus your smart phone camera on this QR code to link directly to a guided meditation commentary on YouTube

God as My Mother

This is perhaps the deepest and most profound relationship I will have with You. In the worldly sense, the mother carries the child in her womb for many months before relationships with others can form from the point of birth. So too, as my Spiritual Mother, You were there to nurture me and to provide a protective environment until I was ready to engage with the world in this new birth.

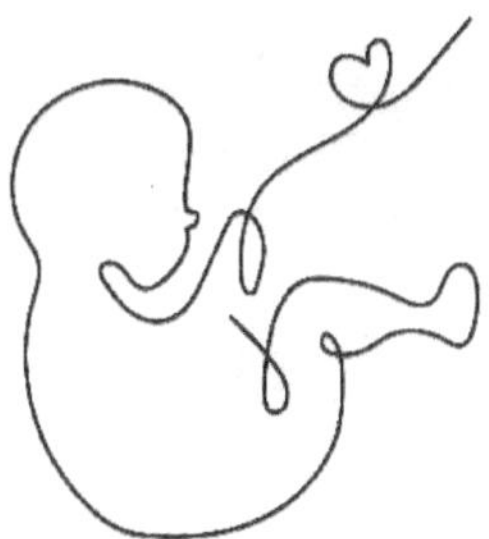

As a small child, You provide me with the feeling of independence because, while remaining close by, You don't tell me what I can and can't do. However, in truth, that place where You left me to play.

You know to be a safe space in which I

experience and grow. In this way, Your protection is incognito and non-intrusive. And when I have explored to my heart's content, I come running back to You – that constant presence with which I feel secure, loved, and nourished.

You are the yin to the Father's yang. You don't give directions and teachings but You do spend time with me doing things together in which, in a very natural manner, You demonstrate the how and why of that task. At other times, when I am upset, You calm me, soothe me, whisper words of encouragement, and offer little signals that dissolve my fears and hurts so that, once again, I can ride forth to do battle with dragons and monsters.

And yet, there are times when You take me completely by surprise, times when You withdraw Your support and Your cooperation. Because this is not the response I expected, I will reflect on this deeply in order to understand why You did what You did. Like this, when I can see the reason behind Your behaviour, the lesson is even more powerful. Once again, You encourage growth within me more by what You refrain from than by what You do.

You are an energy as vast as the ocean, from which I can draw at any moment. The uniqueness and sweetness of this relationship is that because You are always available. I can come to the ocean at the time of need, rather than demanding or expecting the ocean to come to me. In playing this role, You are so incognito.

You are my beautiful Mother.

Focus your smart phone camera on this QR code to link directly to a guided meditation commentary on YouTube

God as My Spiritual Confidante

At the heart of intimacy is the value of trust. It allows me to share my innermost, deepest secrets with You with no recriminations. I can express my deepest thoughts, feelings, fears and concerns without fear of the negative being laughed at or the positive being misunderstood.

Intimacy comes from a place of stability in relationship – whatever details are revealed will not shake the solid foundation, as this foundation is deep and has been built over a long period of time. Intimacy cannot be found in a new relationship.

Like walking on very thick ice, there is a deep-seated knowledge that the ice will, without question, hold my weight and so I step onto it with absolute confidence. If there is any doubt as to the strength of the ice, I will feel my way cautiously, constantly being alert to the possibility of danger and hence, I will be hesitant. Intimacy holds no hesitancy.

Neither does intimacy host regret. Even if You point out to me that my actions were inappropriate or wrong, then it is shared as something to be understood and transformed rather than as a rebuke or a criticism. In fact, our relationship is strengthened rather than compromised.

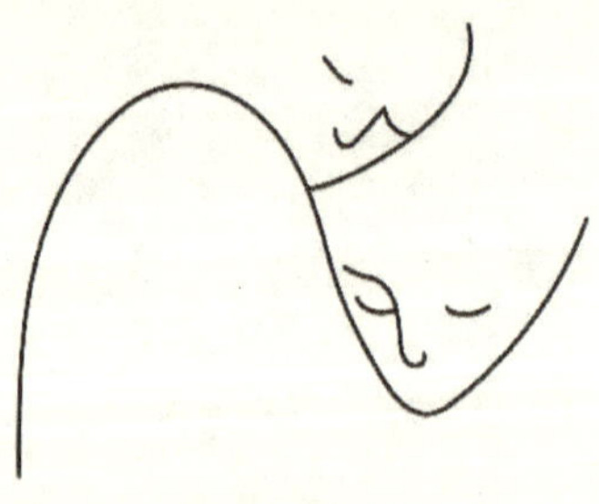

There is a profound sense of comfort in Your presence – even when there may be long periods of silence. That silence doesn't need to be filled with words – there is already an abundance of 'presence.' This is captured in a story of two academics who had worked together for 35 years, one who was now losing the power of speech and the other his hearing. Asked what they would do, one replied, "We will hold hands and there will be a lot of love passing between us. You don't need speech and hearing to feel that!"

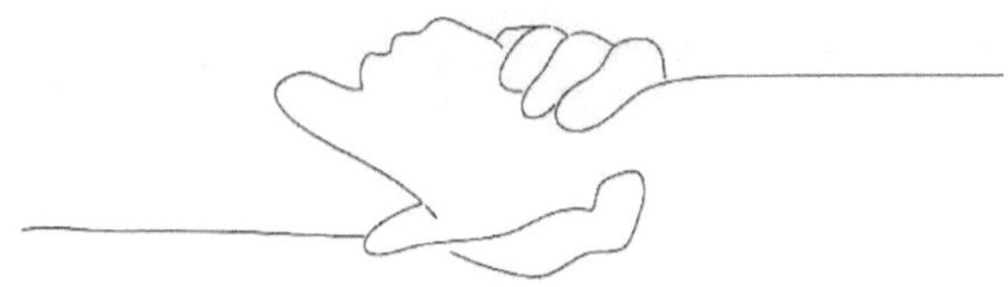

Intimacy provides a security that is not based on You not changing, but one that is based on the recognition of that spiritual core of You not changing – You have demonstrated over a long period of time Your integrity, love, truth, and purity of intent. This is like the well that has been drilled deep into the earth, from which pure water will always be extracted with no possibility of contamination by surface water.

Spiritual intimacy ensures that there will be no idle gossip that contains secrets, shared with You in confidence, being distributed like leaves in the wind – picked up indiscriminately and allowed to blow here and there.

I am safe and secure in Your company.

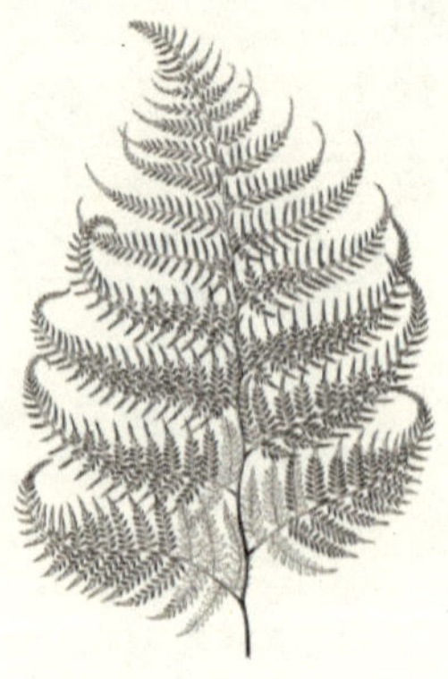

Focus your smart phone camera on this QR code to link directly to a guided meditation commentary on YouTube

God as My Accompanist

When minds meet, they don't just exchange facts; they transform them, reshape them, draw different implications from them and engage in new trains of thought. The art is in the listening. I once read somewhere that the Chinese symbols that make up the word 'listen' are: ear, you, eyes, heart and undivided attention. What could be more apt that this as Your role as the accompanist.

In this relationship, You provide space and opportunity such that my best thoughts are not provided by You but are arrived at by myself. For You, the role of accompanying is an end in itself. You are not looking for some future outcome but are just in the present; just being there; just being!

Your gift is invaluable: not someone who restrains me when I am about to make some mistake, to waste some energy or resource; not someone who gives answers before I have the opportunity to experience it for myself, but someone who bounces my own voice back to me so that I can discover my uniqueness, develop a sense of meaning, and understand my way forward.

In this, You are sensitive, attentive, alert to the themes and ideas which are hidden or partially obscured, finding a way in which to shift my focus to reveal and explore that. Your input is so subtle that I am almost unaware that You have played any part at all.

With time, I realize that I hold the agenda within this relationship and that I invite You into my life. However, as the Ocean of Knowledge, You provide a framework and structure within which I can explore that agenda.

Of course, it should not be overlooked that You, with Your soft heart, which is open and receptive, are always there, ready to respond to such an invitation, always available – the ultimate open-door policy!

Focus your smart phone camera on this QR code to link directly to a guided meditation commentary on YouTube

God as My Choreographer

As the ballerina, You talk me through what is required and I grasp the concept, the technical aspects, the movements. However, it is another thing to execute that, and yet another thing still to do so in a manner that carries the fragrance of natural perfection.

It starts with the mental rehearsal, the visualization, the recognition of the beauty that can be created together. However, it is a journey, a work in progress: sometimes joy, sometimes pain, sometimes hardship, sometimes ease. As with anything of beauty that has to be formed from the raw materials, it requires a repetition of some movement again and again; the hammer striking the red-hot metal in the foundry, the file across the wood in the sculptors' workshop, the laser polishing the facets of the diamond.

Practice; refinement, perfection.

Practice; refinement, perfection.

That is our task together: You standing back ... silent ... observing ... noting the smallest correction that will bring benefit to the artistic expression.

There is never any sign of inappropriateness or

incongruence of movement, for the experience You bring carries with it a quiet, all-knowing confidence. From my part, You chose your dancer with care for You know my innate capacity to bend, to stretch, to reach the heights that will convey just what a masterpiece You created.

Those who watch are not drawn to one particular move or another for the flow is seamless - the physical manifestation beautifully synchronized with the emotional and spiritual expression. I am one with the dance and the dance is a mirror of myself.

But I wish to draw attention to something ... actually, someone. You! Your humility is such that the applause, the praise, and maybe even the adulation come to me, the ballerina, and not to You, the Choreographer, the One who masterminded the performance so quietly, so subtly, so incognito. I accept the applause but, in my heart, I acknowledge You are the inspiration behind the scenes.

As with anything that expresses perfection, it inspires others to either follow, to draw it to the attention of another, or just to keep it close to their heart, to return to at a time of imagination and dreaming of one's own potential. Perfection never goes unnoticed.

Focus your smart phone camera on this QR code to link directly to a guided meditation commentary on YouTube

God as My Best Friend

What makes You my best friend?

When I am in Your company we are inseparable, but my happiness is not dependent upon that company. Neither is it dependent upon the words we exchange, for I know that sometimes words spoken in haste carry hurt – not that <u>You</u> do anything in haste. Such words are always forgiven and forgotten. Why?

The foundation, the bedrock of our relationship is that of respect and this can never be eroded: the surface may show cracks or scarring but this has always proved, with time, to be inconsequential.

When I call You at a time of need, You drop everything and come immediately – not when it suits You but when it suits me. In fact, You put my well-being in front of all else. Consequently, my trust in You is absolute. I know that if I were to close my eyes and let myself fall backwards – even at the last possible moment – You would be there to catch me. My faith and confidence in You is unquestioning.

I know that in sharing my deepest secrets and fears You will not think any less of me because You know the motive and intent behind my every action. Our relationship, developed over years, means that our understanding of each other is natural and intuitive; the smallest signal carries chapters of experience.

It is all of this together that makes this relationship such a 'good read.'

Focus your smart phone camera on this QR code to link directly to a guided meditation commentary on YouTube

Reflection

As human beings, we thrive when in relationship. Our search for love, peace and happiness takes us out into the world of relationships and eventually back inside ourselves. As you read these personal reflections about a relationship with God:

Which relationship resonated most for you?

When you reflect on your relationship with God, what qualities do you experience?

Which relationship would you like to explore more?

A Connection with God

God is a sentient being of spiritual light. The energy of this Divine Light is pure benevolence radiating love, peace and spiritual power to all souls of the world. God sees each soul as a precious diamond-like child.

The simple practice of meditation links the soul directly to the Supreme Being.

Raja Yoga Meditation as taught by the Brahma Kumaris centres worldwide will help you connect with the Divine Source.

The organization is an international non-governmental organization that offers all its courses and programs for free. The organization is administered by women.

For more information, or to contact a meditation centre near you, visit www.brahmakumaris.org

And check out **thelighthouse.world** for wonderful resources!

www.ingramcontent.com/pod-product-compliance
Lightning Source LLC
La Vergne TN
LVHW041259150826
845673LV00008B/2661

* 9 7 9 8 8 9 6 3 2 8 5 5 1 *